HOW TO DRAW CARTOONS

Peter Coupe

ARCTURUS

Published by Arcturus Publishing Limited
for Bookmart Limited
Registered Number 2372865
Trading as Bookmart Limited
Desford Road
Enderby
Leicester
LE9 5AD

This Edition Published 1997

Printed and bound in Slovakia

© Peter Coupe/Arcturus Publishing Limited

ISBN - 1 900032 81 3

Contents

Introduction

What materials you need to get started.
How, where and when to work.
How to get the best from this book.

Yes, I know you're straining at the leash to have a go, but please read this section first, so that you get into good working habits right from the start, and you know exactly what this book is going to do for you!

What you need to get started

One of the great things about cartoon drawing is the fact that you probably have everything you need to make a start already, so you don't actually need to go out and spend any money.

You can certainly make a start with more or less any pen or pencil that comes to hand, and you can draw on just about anything. The great painter L.S. Lowry painted on flattened-out cardboard boxes.

My own first published cartoon was drawn in ballpoint pen on the back of a discarded shoe box.

If you are serious about your cartoon drawing you will almost certainly want to buy your own 'special' set of drawing materials and equipment. It needn't be expensive to buy everything you need to start, and you can add to your basic kit as the need arises, or when you feel the desire to experiment If you do decide to buy your own set of equipment for cartoon drawing then I would suggest you start with the following...

...a couple of pencils; grade 'B' or '2B' are the best because you can rub them out without leaving marks on the paper. The harder grades of pencil ('H', '2H', '3H' and so on) can damage the paper surface. The softer grades of pencil ('3B', '4B' and up to '9B') will smudge more, and you will be constantly rubbing out marks on the paper and washing the smudge marks off your hands.

A pencil eraser is an essential, both for removing mistakes and also for removing 'guidelines' from your finished drawings. I use a soft 'plastic' eraser and find this works well for me.

A pencil sharpener is also vital for keeping a good point on your pencils. A metal one will cost more, but will usually last longer than plastic, and is far less likely to break when you stand on it. Some sharpeners also have replaceable blades, and some people even use electric-powered ones!

I'll bet you never thought that pencil sharpeners could lead such an exciting life.

Pens come in an amazing variety of colours, shapes and sizes. Ballpoint pens are quite handy to carry around for sketching, but steer clear of cheap ones which tend to blotch and blob on the page, especially when they get warm.

Felt and fibre tipped pens are also easy to carry and use, but the ink in these pens can be 'fugitive' sometimes.

This means that the drawings can fade or change colour in a relatively short time, and the ink can sometimes spread out and blur.

Technical pens are excellent, and are very high quality items that will last for many years.

These pens are quite expensive, but they will last a long time providing you keep them clean. I have a couple of pens more than twenty years old that are still going strong.

I mainly use the 0.6 and the 0.8 sizes.

You can also experiment with inexpensive fountain pens, old fashioned 'dip' pens and artists' sketching pens.

A visit to your local art or graphic design supplies shop will enable you to see what is on offer.

Remember to look after your pens, and clean them after use.

Brushes are also used by most cartoonists at some stage. Some will do all their drawing and lettering with a brush; others will use brushes for filling in areas of solid black in a drawing. A size 6 brush should be large enough for most 'filling in' and a size 2 or 4 for experiments with drawing and lettering. Sable brushes are the best quality and should last the longest; but they are the most expensive. There are plenty of cheaper nylon brushes that will give good service. Again, a visit to the art shop will enable you to have a good look at what is on offer and to compare prices and quality.

Paper comes in a bewildering variety of sizes, surface finishes, colours and weights, but to make life simple I advise you to use inexpensive white typing or photocopying paper. This has a fairly smooth surface, and if you ask for a weight of about 80gsm that will be more than sufficient for most of your work.

A ream (500 sheets) of this paper can be purchased quite inexpensively from a discount stationers and will last you for a good long time.

You will, from time to time, make mistakes – we all do! However, don't despair and throw the drawing into the waste basket, because you can cover over most mistakes and carry on drawing. Small errors can be hidden with typing correction fluid.

Larger mistakes can be patched over with a piece of paper, cut to shape, and pasted over with a glue stick or something similar. When the glue is dry you just continue the drawing over the patch. If you photocopy the finished drawing the edge of the patch will not show up.

(Patching is quite a common practice among cartoonists and illustrators, so don't worry if you end up having to do it from time to time.)

PATCH

THIS EDGE WILL NOT SHOW

How, where and when to work

I think that the best way to learn anything is to begin with the 'little and often' method. This means that, wherever possible, you set aside a short period of time every day for your cartoon work: 10 or 15 minutes will be sufficient in the beginning, but if you can do it every day, or almost every day, you will soon find your cartoon drawing skills growing.

You will progress far better doing a small amount each day than you would leaving it all week and then having a marathon 2 or 3 hour session on one day a week.

Try to find a regular place to work and, if at all possible, make this the place where you keep all your drawing equipment as well. You can fit everything you need to draw cartoons into a small box.

Different people have different needs when drawing cartoons. Some people can work in a noisy kitchen, among all the rest of the family comings and goings. Others (like me!) prefer a quiet space, where the only sound is the scratching of a pen nib across paper, and maybe the low mumble of a radio somewhere in the background.

Although I have a studio now, with everything conveniently to hand, I started drawing on a rickety old dressing table in the corner of a bedroom.

It was the furthest corner from the window and I could hear the neighbours arguing through the walls, which at least gave me some ideas for cartoons!

The only light I had was a 15-watt strip light, which invariably left me with a headache and eye strain; so I would strongly advise you to make sure you have plenty of light right from the start, either from a window or a reading lamp, or both.

You can fit your lamp with a 'daylight' or blue bulb, to make it more like real daylight – a lot easier on the eyes.

The time of day you work will depend on your own personal free time. You might be an early riser and choose to work first thing in the morning, while the rest of the family are trying to get started. If you're a night owl you can work, as I tend to, in that very quiet time between 11 pm and 1 am. Some people I know work on the bus or tube, others in the lunch beak, or even in the bath.

Don't worry if you want to work in secret at first; you won't feel confident about showing other people your drawings. But this will pass, and you will be able to draw more easily when you stop worrying about whether people see what you are doing. In my experience the vast majority of family and friends are incredibly supportive of budding cartoonists and are a great source of encouragement.

Be warned – it won't be long before they want cartoons for Birthday presents!

How to get the best from this book

'How To Draw Cartoons' is a complete cartoon drawing course in a single book.

It is probably a good idea to read fairly quickly through the whole book, and then go back to the start and read each chapter in more detail, and try out the exercises as you go along. There is no right or wrong amount of time you should take to work through the book: whatever feels most comfortable and enjoyable for you is right.

At the end of each chapter there is an assignment and a 'workout' for you to complete to consolidate the new things you have learned from the chapter.

Each assignment is designed to build on the one before, so that you are learning new skills that you can integrate with the things you have learned already.

For this reason it is a good idea to work through the book in sequence. When you have finished the book you will find it an invaluable reference source, and you will be able to look back and refresh yourself whenever the need arises.

You can repeat different assignments in the book as often as you like, and even repeat the whole book every 6 months if you really want to see how much you've improved!

Remember to keep everything you draw – no matter how tempted you are to screw it up and throw it in the wastepaper basket – so that you can compare the standard and quality of your very first cartoons with the ones you produce later. You will be surprised, even amazed, at the amount of improvement in your drawing ability that you will achieve with even a small amount of regular practice.

Don't be discouraged by any early setbacks and failures you might encounter. You will quickly develop your own way of working; and as your abilities grow, so will your confidence.

ASSIGNMENT

Collect together a small set of basic cartoon drawing materials and equipment. Start with a pencil or two, an eraser and sharpener, a few pens, a glue stick for patching mistakes, and maybe a brush or two and a bottle of ink.

Some photocopying or typing paper will see you 'fully equipped' and ready to start.

Earmark a place to work, and set about making it as bright and comfortable as you can.

Now try this simple workout...

1   Draw a question mark on a blank sheet of paper.
2   Now draw a number 3 a little to the right of it, and a second number 3, back to front, a little to the left of it.
3   Draw a curved line a little above the question mark, and another curved line a little below it.
4   Draw a straight line from the bottom of the number 3 to a place just above the curved line; do the same with the back-to-front number 3.
5   Draw a big, sweeping curve from the top of the number 3 to the top of the back-to-front number 3.
6   Draw a series of dashes along the base of the drawing, between the straight lines.
7   Draw two semi-circles on top of the nearest curve, and put a dot in the middle of each one.
8   Turn the drawing round and see your first cartoon drawing!

Pictures of Matchstick Men

Drawing the easiest cartoon figure of all.
Draw a cartoon with 5 blobs and 11 sticks.
Action.
Proportion.
What size to draw.

Drawing the easiest cartoon figure of all

The stick figure is something we are all familiar with, although we probably haven't drawn one since childhood. The stick figure gives us a basic set of proportions for a typical, albeit skinny, human body shape.

If I handed you a blank sheet of paper and asked you to draw a cartoon figure on it you might well be a little daunted by the prospect; but if I asked you to draw a matchstick figure you would almost certainly be able to do it – with a reasonable degree of confidence. Using the stick figure gives us a basis for drawing the complete cartoon figure.

So, before we go any further, I want you to do just that. Draw a couple of matchstick figures on a spare piece of paper, and then read on.

There is a pretty good chance that your matchstick figure looks something like the ones that I've drawn here.

Note that the shoulder and hip 'bones' or sticks can only be seen from the front. When you are looking at the figure from the side they are not seen. Check this in a mirror as you draw.

Draw a cartoon with 5 blobs and 11 sticks...

Look at this drawing: 11 sticks for the various 'bones' in the body, and 5 blobs for the hands, feet and head. There is a pretty good chance that your matchstick figure looks something like the one that I've drawn here.

Now that we know what parts we need to construct our basic figure we can use this to draw a basic human shape in any position using this simple system.

Great, isn't it?

What's more, you can actually make one of these figures and just move the various parts around to get the 'action' that you need.

Use drinking straws, cocktail sticks, spent matches or even pencils to construct the figure on a suitable flat surface; then copy the lines onto your drawing paper. For something a little more permanent you could make a stick figure from strips of thick card joined with paper fasteners.

When you draw a stick figure, remember to leave a gap where one 'bone' goes behind another. The bone in front stays solid; the one behind has the gap.

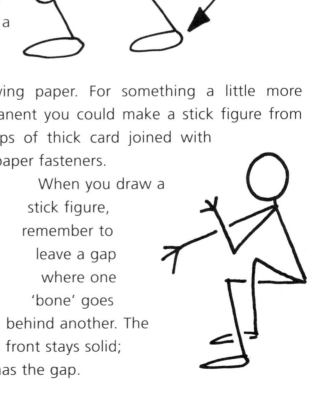

BLOBS

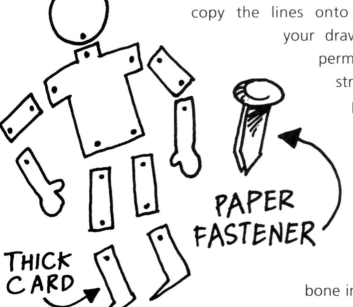

THICK CARD

PAPER FASTENER

Why not have a try at this right now? Find something to make your own essential cartoon matchstick figure, and draw a couple of dozen poses for yourself, just to prove it really works!

Action

While we are at this stage it is worth reminding yourself that it is important to think of your little figures as action figures. You can make them do anything you want to on the page – no sitting around watching TV for this lot: take them to the limit and back again!

Below I have assembled a gallery of figures in action to get you started.

Fill up a few dozen sheets of that typing paper you bought with these stick figures. Refer back to your model as you go along, and try out as many poses as you can think of.

Proportion

The figures we are drawing are pretty normal at this stage. The halfway point on the figure is around the waist, and the arms finish just below hip height. The head will divide into the body about 5 times. The hips and shoulders (which we can see if we look at our stick figure from the front) are about the same width across.

But suppose we want to deliberately exaggerate one or other feature; for example, suppose we want a character with a big head on a small body, or an ape with long arms, or a super-hero figure with huge shoulders.

Well, now we have our basic stick figure we can do any of those things, and many more, with a flick of the pen (or brush)!

Look at this selection of odd shapes and sizes. Arms, legs, bodies or just about anything else can all be longer, shorter, fatter or thinner to suit the mood and activity of your cartoon characters.

You will learn about drawing all the other essential bits and pieces that make up a cartoon person as we work through this book, but remember that the stick figure is the most important part of the drawing, because it gives you the structure to build everything else on – with confidence!

Make sure you practise these sketchy skeletons regularly. They are going to be a great help to you in many of the other drawing projects to come, and they are especially useful in situations where you don't have a lot of room to hold the action – as in a strip cartoon or comic book page.

CAPTAIN... CC ...CARTOON !

What size to draw

This is a simple enough question, but it seems to worry an awful lot of newcomers to cartooning. To some extent the answer is 'whatever size you like', but if I suggest that you start drawing figures about the size of the one I have drawn after this paragraph you probably won't go far wrong.

If at any time you find yourself yearning to draw larger or smaller figures, then you should follow your own leanings and do just that.

I usually work on an A4 sized sheet of paper, with each complete drawing taking up about half the actual paper surface, with large margins all the way round my drawing.

Remember that the larger your work the more space there will be for detail in your cartoon drawing. You will also need to use a finer pen to get detail in smaller drawings. It's all pretty logical really, and some simple experiments will soon have you on the right track. Eventually you will develop a formula that is just right for you. Time for another assignment and 'work-out' session...

ASSIGNMENT

Construct a couple of real stick figures to help your drawing. Use spent matches, cocktail sticks or whatever else comes to hand. Fill a few sheets of paper with stick figures running, jumping, throwing, catching, playing golf, football, cricket, hockey, tennis, etc., etc.

Try some drawings with exaggerated proportions – longer arms or legs, smaller or larger bodies, small and large figures together, for example.

Now try this simple workout...

Take the letters of the alphabet and incorporate them into stick figures. Look at the examples below to see what you are aiming at.

Use letters with straight lines first, as they will be easier – L and T and F, for example, and then try out some of the trickier ones with curves – B, R, Q and S might prove interesting!

Face Values

Make your cartoon faces come alive.
How to show emotion and expression.
How to draw men and women, children and oldies.
Cartoon shorthand.

Make your cartoon faces come alive

People looking at your cartoons will look at the faces you create as a clue to what is going on in the cartoon. Look at these two faces. One of them is saying, 'I've lost my contact lens.' It should be easy to see which. Matching the emotion in the cartoon to the face you actually draw is the next task.

(Of course, you might want to deliberately have the 'wrong' look on the face of one of your characters, which is fine. But make sure you know which face you are going to put on your little people, and why.)

You don't need to add a whole lot of detail to make a cartoon face do its job: far from it. In fact, the less cluttered a face is, the easier it is to read the expression.

People only look at a cartoon for a very short space of time, and you must get the idea across to them in that short time. They will rarely linger to try and puzzle out what you have tried to do; they only want what they can get from it at a glance.

Take out a small mirror and try out some different faces. Just look at your face in the mirror for a couple of seconds, and then write down the two most important features.

If you noted the eyes and the mouth, well done!

Let's look at ways of using them.

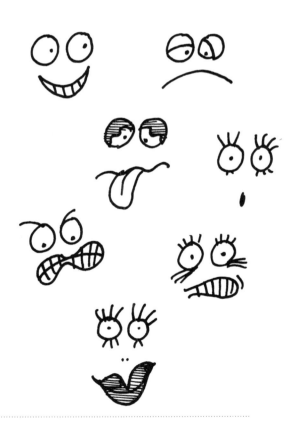

How to show emotion and expression

Let's use this mirror some more in this next section. As I can't be sitting next to you to show you exactly what I mean I will have to rely on your own 'face-pulling' abilities. Do this behind locked doors if you feel a bit self-conscious.

Look into your mirror and smile. Don't show your teeth, just smile with your lips, as though your boss has just told you a very old joke, but you don't want to upset him/her too much by not falling over with mirth.

Draw an oval head shape to put the face into, about the size of a large egg will do for now, and draw an upside down question mark in the middle of the egg for a nose. We will do lots of different noses (and eyes and ears and teeth and everything else) as we go along, but this will get you started. Now, draw that simple face. Just use simple oval or round shapes for eyes, mouth, eyebrows, and ears.

When you have finished, let's check to see if we agree on the basic characteristics of this fairly happy face.

Upward curving smiley mouth, wide open eyes, eyebrows above eyes, maybe as shown even some little cheeks showing at the ends of the mouth. Well, that wasn't too difficult, was it?

Now add the open mouth and teeth to this face. Just draw three curved lines, instead of one for the mouth, that all meet at the ends. Draw a series of straight lines (like railings) down from top to bottom to show the teeth. Now your boss has just told you that you are going to get a 20% pay rise.

See how much more expressive this face is.

Let's change the eyes around a little now. Keep the mouth smiling with the teeth showing, but now make the eyes look out from these down-angled eyebrows. This is a face that is clearly up to something, I think you'll agree. A really sneaky face.

Maybe the boss has just promised to make you assistant manager, if only you can think of some way of getting rid of old Blenkinsop first...

Now let's change the mouth around again, but keep those sinister eyes. I hope you are remembering to check these expressions in the mirror from time to time.

Let's make an angry mouth now – just draw a figure of 8 lying on its side. Add the 'railings' as you did for the smiling face to give a set of teeth, although you can always block a few of these out if you ever draw a pirate or similar 'baddie'.

And let's add a little shading to the cheeks under the eyes – where you are now turning crimson because Blenkinsop has just announced that he intends to buy the company, make himself chairman and appoint his niece as assistant manager!

Let's go back to the happy eyes again, with eyebrows high in the top of the head. This time the mouth moves into a downward curve, making a thoroughly miserable face. Blenkinsop has just downgraded you to a mail room clerk!

In the last face in this set let's keep the sad mouth, but replace the eyes with the sinister ones from the plotting and angry faces we have just drawn (3 and 4).

Still unhappy, but this time thinking of ways to get even. This is the 'I'm not taking this lying down!' face.

There are lots more faces you can construct, and a few minutes experimenting with the mirror will doubtless reveal many of them to you.

Here are a few more for you to try out for yourself; feel free to mix and match the various bits and pieces to get the face you're after.

How to draw men and women, children and oldies

I know it is dangerous to generalise in these politically correct times, but I'm going to anyway! Generally, women have longer hair than men, and they generally wear more lipstick, and they generally use more nail varnish and are generally more likely to wear dresses.

On the other hand, men are generally more likely to be found wearing suits, with bald(ing) heads, and wearing very little in the way of eye make-up, nail varnish or lipstick.

If any of the above still offends anyone, I think they are reading the wrong book!

So take a look at this basic face and see how I have 'converted' it to both a male and a female face in the drawings below by simply adding some of the attributes mentioned above.

When drawing oldies, like me, you have rather more to go at. Wrinkles are the first thing you might notice, followed closely by a slight shortage in the hair department! A definite increase in girth might well be allowed, or perhaps a willowy thinness, depending on the sort of person you are drawing. Hairstyles change, as do clothes, headgear and accessories.

Very, very old people are usually drawn rather wiry and stooped, and are seen wearing astonishingly moth-eaten cardigans – though they can, by the magic of cartooning, still run faster, jump further and drink more beer than anyone a quarter their age!

Children are small and round. Their heads are sometimes not much smaller than their bodies, and their features are small and placed more in the centre of the face.

These 'rules' are not, of course, rigid – they are merely a guide to get you started.

If you want to produce a cartoon strip of 'Super Granny' and her sidekick 'Infant Boy' then you go ahead, and don't let anyone stop you.

Cartoon shorthand

Cartoon shorthand is a way of indicating what is happening without using words.

It is a way of 'showing' rather than 'telling'.

In this face we have all the cartoon hallmarks of anger: beads of sweat flying everywhere, shaded cheeks to show how flushed they are, shake lines around the head and body, fists clenched and steam coming out of the ears.

Cartoonists still use the good old light bulb for an idea, a question mark for puzzlement and an exclamation mark to show annoyance or indignation. Wiggly lines show that it is hot or smelly and jagged lines usually indicate a definite case of electric shock treatment!

Speed lines show that someone is moving quickly, as do little puffs of smoke; drawn simply as three lines, the number 33 and then two smaller lines.

When someone is really travelling they are usually portrayed actually off the ground, with a little shadow on the ground below them to emphasise the action. Generally speaking, the faster a character is travelling, the further forward they lean.

Echoes show where someone has been but is no longer. Useful for showing a quick turn of the head or rapid movement like falling.

So even before our little people actually say anything, we can convey a lot of what is happening in the cartoon by signs and symbols like these.

ASSIGNMENT

Draw a complete collection of faces in various stages of anger, happiness, puzzlement, surprise and misery.

Draw a few faces changing from one emotional state to another, as we did in the last chapter, and construct a short story about what is happening.

Now try this simple workout...

Use the letters of the alphabet again, this time to construct faces. Have a look at the examples given below, and try some out for yourself. It should, in theory, be possible to use every letter of the alphabet in this way, and it is, in fact, a very good way to sharpen up your creative face-drawing skills.

Hands and Feet

Drawing simple hands and feet.
Adding more detail.
Movement in hands and feet.

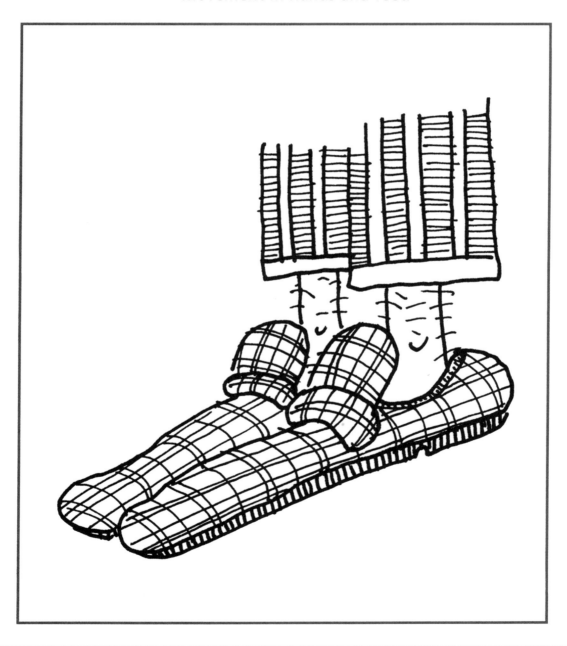

Drawing simple hands and feet

Remember that hands and feet, far from being the inconvenient blobs at the ends of the arms and legs, can be used as an integral part of the cartoon itself.

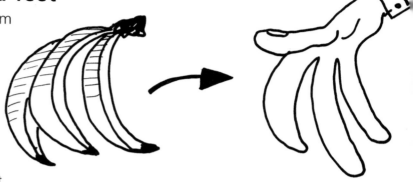

Hands especially can be used to express emotions and give directions. If a cartoon figure points at something in the cartoon, then you are certain to look where he or she is pointing. You can exaggerate the action and even the size of hands in your cartoon to get the desired effect.

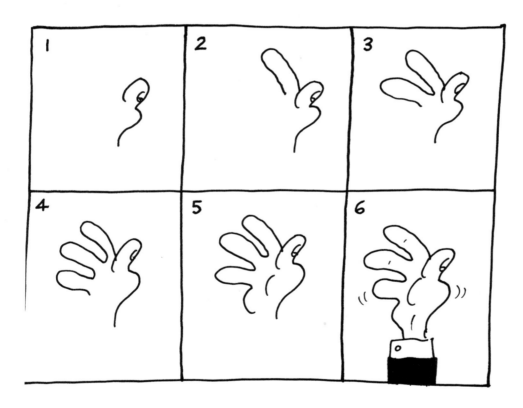

Let's start with some simple hand shapes...

...A bunch of bananas is a pretty good starting point.

Turn the banana stalk into the cuff of a shirt or blouse, round off the fingers a little, add some sort of thumb shape, and we're nearly there.

The sequence of 6 drawings below shows how I would construct a hand – not a million miles from the bananas really, is it?

Start with the thumb and the soft thumb 'pad', then add fingers one at a time, and then the other side of the hand, the wrist and the cuff.

This could easily be a waving hand if it is drawn vertically, or a hand held out for a handshake drawn horizontally. If it is the back of the hand, you can show this easily by missing out the thumb 'pad' and instead adding a fingernail or two.

Little curls show a finger bent into the palm, as in a pointing finger or a fist. Again, to show this from the back, simply leave out the details of the inside of the hand.

Check – using a mirror – that you have the thumbs in the right place. With your hands by your sides the thumbs point forward and the fingers curl in slightly.

With a hand outstretched (to shake hands) the thumb is on top and points upwards.

You can have thin pointy fingers or short stubby ones. Remember that they will have an effect on the character you are drawing, so choose something appropriate, unless you want to deliberately mislead people.

FRONT

BACK

The most important thing to remember about feet is that they have a heel.

After that you can do pretty much what you want with them. The heel is important because it helps to 'balance' the foot, both in reality and in the cartoon. A foot without a heel is a foot always on the verge of toppling over.

You can get away with really very simple foot shapes, like these. Add detail if you want to, and remember that feet can be in slippers and flippers as well as ordinary footwear.

They can also be great fun with nothing on them at all!

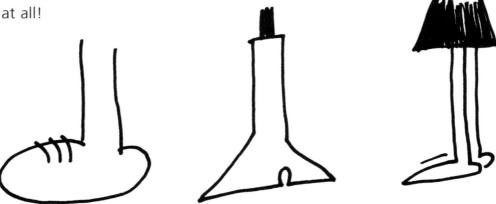

BIG TOE
POINTS
UP

Remember that the big toe is on the inside, and that the big toe points upwards, while all the other toes point down.

If all else fails, and you find drawing hands and feet impossible, just draw all your cartoons of people standing in the sea with their hands in their pockets.

Adding more detail

Some cartoonists are quite happy to stay with the bunch-of-bananas hand and the blob feet for ever. As long as it does the job, they insist, why bother with more detail? You may feel the same way yourself, or you might want to embellish your drawings with tons of completely surplus – but very satisfying – little extras.

It will, of course, be easier to add detail to a larger drawing than a smaller one. You really have to decide for yourself where you stop. Look at the work of other cartoonists and see which style appeals to you most. Some will draw with a few brisk strokes of the pen (or pencil), while others spend a lot of time getting every stitch and wrinkle just right.

Movement in hands and feet

Don't allow your beautifully drawn hands and feet to hang limp at the sides of your cartoon character – make them part of the action!

   Remember that hands can wave, punch, slap, grab, tickle, throw, catch, carry and swim (to name but a few possibilities)

and feet can ski, kick, cycle, be tickled, jog, run and hop (to name but a few others).

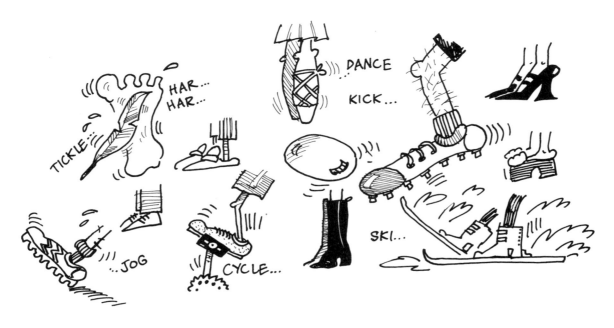

ASSIGNMENT

Fill a few pages with hands and feet of various shapes and sizes. Try hands with four fingers as well as three and decide which suits you best. Try some combination pictures, where the hands and the face can be seen together – try to match the moods of the faces with appropriate hand gestures.

Now try this workout...

Select half a dozen of your favourite cartoons, by yourself or other cartoonists, and redraw them using just hands as the drawn part of the cartoon, and keeping the words the same.

BUT IF YOU DIDN'T ASK ME
QUESTIONS I WOULDN'T
HAVE TO TELL YOU LIES!

DON'T WORRY – THESE
NEW SPECTACLES ARE
REALLY GOOD!

RACE YOU
TO THE
POST.
OFFICE...

Dressing Up

Easy ways to add clothes to your simple stick figures.
Drawing men and women.
Uniform.

Easy ways to add clothes to your simple stick figures

The task of moving from a stick figure to a fully finished cartoon character may seem a little daunting at first, but rest assured there are simple ways to enable you to do it with a minimum of fuss.

Just as we relied on simple sticks for the figure shape, we will now rely on simple blob shapes to help us construct the rest of the character.

In this drawing I have drawn over my original stick figure with rough pencil blobs to give a feel for the clothed shape of the figure. I have left the stick figure in the drawing as a series of dashes to avoid confusion.

Using a bit of cartoon 'shorthand' I can now add features like shirt collar, tie, lapels, and so on. Now the cartoon figure begins to take shape.

(At this stage I would normally sketch in the head and facial features, hands and feet. If I was happy that all the elements of the drawing were coming together I would draw over my rough sketch in ink, making any final corrections and additions as I go along).

Try some of these for yourself and see how you get on. Stay loose and relaxed and just sketch your ideas in place. Draw a few stick figures in black ink on a sheet of paper and draw your finished figures on sheets of tracing paper laid over it. This will save you having to re-draw and rub out the stick figure shapes.

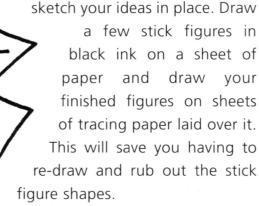

SHIRT COLLAR, TIE AND LAPELS ARE SIMPLE TRIANGLE SHAPES !

Drawing Men and Women

Have a look at the basic stick figure below, and then at the two figures, one male and one female, that have been derived from it.

Start out by drawing the rather obvious stuff like women in blouses and skirts, men in suits and ties.

As you get better at cartooning and learn to employ your observation more, you will be able to draw anyone wearing anything – with complete confidence.

Don't stop at men in suits and women in dresses, though; try pink-headed punks, Amazonian Indians, pop stars, Eskimos, Martians and anything else that comes to mind.

Uniform

One important element in cartooning is uniform. Lots of people wear uniform, and it makes life a lot easier if you learn to draw a few for yourself.

Police officer, train driver, teacher in traditional cap and gown (yes, I know

very few people wear them these days – that's not the point, this is a book on cartooning, and in the cartoon world they all do), burglar in striped shirt, loot bag and face mask (see note above), jockey, butcher, waiter, waitress and traffic warden should keep you going for the time being.

You will find yourself inventing appropriate characters as your own cartooning preferences start to 'take over' your drawing.

A lot of my cartoons have vintage car enthusiasts, photographers, tubby bespectacled old(er) men and other incarnations of me in them!

ASSIGNMENT

Draw the same couple as babies, teenagers, adults and oldies. Note how you change the clothes, hair, posture and accessories to make the change in them.

Draw a group of the same type of people – schoolteachers, business men and women, hippies, punks, builders, for example. Given that they all do the same job, how do you make them different?

Try a few slightly more unusual characters: A Chinese Mandarin or an Amazonian Indian for example.

Now try this workout...

Prepare a piece of thin card as shown below. Cut along the dotted lines. Draw one character on the inside centre section, and another two on the side flaps. By folding each flap over one another you can create a startling number of funny combinations.

Settings and Props

How to draw backgrounds in a few strokes.
Adding props to help the joke along.
Zooming in on the important action.

How to draw backgrounds in a few strokes

The important thing to remember about backgrounds in cartoons is that they are there to help the action along, not to be a masterpiece that distracts from what the cartoon people are doing and saying.

A common mistake that newcomers to cartooning often make is to try and put too much into the background in the mistaken belief that a highly detailed background will somehow enhance the cartoon itself. What actually happens is that the background becomes cluttered.

Ideally you should produce a background that 'suggests' the place and time that the cartoon is set in, but still leaves plenty of room for the imagination of the person looking at the cartoon to fill in any gaps.

The two cartoons that follow are both set in a pub or bar. Look at the first cartoon and see how the interior is hinted at with just a few essential details; the beer pumps, ashtray, glasses, and the bar itself.

In the second drawing I have added much more detail. I think you will agree the first drawing is more satisfactory as you can see 'at a glance' what is happening and where. In the

second drawing the characters seem to disappear beneath a mountain of detail – none of which is needed to make the cartoon 'work'.

Collect photographs of a variety of locations and keep them in a loose-leaf folder. Use them to construct a variety of settings, and practise drawing these settings at regular intervals, always striving for a simple but instantly recognisable location as the end result.

If you feel confident enough you can sit and sketch in a variety of 'real' locations, which is useful if you intend to produce cartoons for friends, family or co-workers, as they will recognise these real places. You will also notice that I have kept the drawing 'flat' as far as possible, and haven't shown any table tops or perspective in either drawing.

Perspective is another thing that seems to frighten budding cartoonists, and is almost completely avoidable if you think about it for a moment or two before you start to draw.

The trick to remember is that you see the tops of things if you are above them, and the bottom if you are below them. The further above you are, the more of the top you will see, and the further below you are, the more bottom you will see.

If you try to draw from what I call the 'armchair' position you won't go far wrong, and you can experiment with some simple perspective drawing when you feel a little more confident.

The 'armchair' position simply means that you should draw everything as though you are sitting in an armchair. This way you see a minimum of tops and bottoms and your drawing problems should be few and far between.

There is no doubt that a variety of angles and viewpoints can greatly enhance your cartoon drawings, but they should be incorporated in your drawings only when you feel confident enough to tackle them without fear!

Two views that you can safely experiment with are

WORM'S EYE VIEW

BIRD'S EYE VIEW

shown here; the 'bird's eye view' and the 'worm's eye view'.

These are both quite extreme distortions, but they look good when used with care, and will hopefully encourage you to experiment with perspective and distortion in your own cartoons.

Start with a lightly drawn pencil triangle, and fit the action inside this; you characters will then get

smaller the nearer you place them to the point of the triangle – which is exactly what we want! You can use this perspective trick sideways as well to good effect.

Adding props to help the joke along

You should always try to give your cartoon people something to do, otherwise there is the danger that you will drift towards the 'talking heads' type of cartoon which is a pretty lifeless affair and can almost be set on a rubber stamp with just a space left for a different caption each time you draw. Learn to draw cameras, computers, mobile phones, and anything else that someone in one of your cartoons might pick up and use. This is especially important in cartoons about hobbies and pastimes. Make sure you get things right – because there is always an expert somewhere waiting to correct you.

Make things bigger, too. Things can safely be two or three times their 'real' size in a cartoon, especially if someone is going to get hit by them!

Learn to draw something new every day if you can, and keep all these drawings in a small notebook or sketchbook for reference. It is very time-consuming, for example, having to dig out a photographic magazine to help with a drawing of a camera that forms a minor part of the finished cartoon. Far better to have a sketch to hand or, better still, a variety of sketches.

Don't be afraid to tackle anything. After all, no-one needs to see your 'failures' but you, and it is very frustrating having to abandon a great idea for a cartoon simply because you can't draw a particular prop.

Set yourself tasks – draw something

beginning with each letter of the alphabet each day.
Today is A – Aardvark, tomorrow is B – Butterfly,
and so on.

When you get to the end – start again!

Deliberately draw things you find difficult –
break them down into smaller parts if this helps, or
use matchsticks and blobs to help
you dissect them.

Zooming in on the important action

As well as leaving
unnecessary
detail out of your
cartoons to make
them work better,
you also need to leave out
any extraneous background
material. When you are enjoying
working on a particularly good
drawing, it is all too easy to widen the
picture to include too much material.

Trim the drawing down to the 'active' part of the cartoon,
leaving out anything which doesn't contribute to the joke.

This saves someone having to search around the drawing to find
the actual point of the joke, and it also saves you a whole lot of
drawing time. Doing this will almost always increase the size of the
figures in your cartoon – as you will normally be cutting off lots of
unnecessary background – which in turn should make your cartoon
people easier to draw.

ASSIGNMENT

Fill a few sheets of paper with drawings of objects. Start with the contents of one room in your house. Don't draw large, or with great amounts of detail; keep everything simple and quick.

Draw three or four different backgrounds. Pick subjects that you don't know well – otherwise it would be easy, and we can't have that!

Collect a file of magazine cut-outs of things (kettles, teapots, motorcycles, oven gloves, lampshades, etc.) and places for reference, and draw some of these from the photographs you have collected.

Draw objects in varying sizes and practise making them larger in your cartoons to see the effect.

Now try this workout...

Have someone collect half a dozen small items for you and place them in a shoe box. Now feel each of these items and try to draw them from your sense of touch alone. Compare the objects to your drawings when you have drawn them all.

Drawing Techniques

Drawing in various media.
Adding texture and shading.
Lettering.

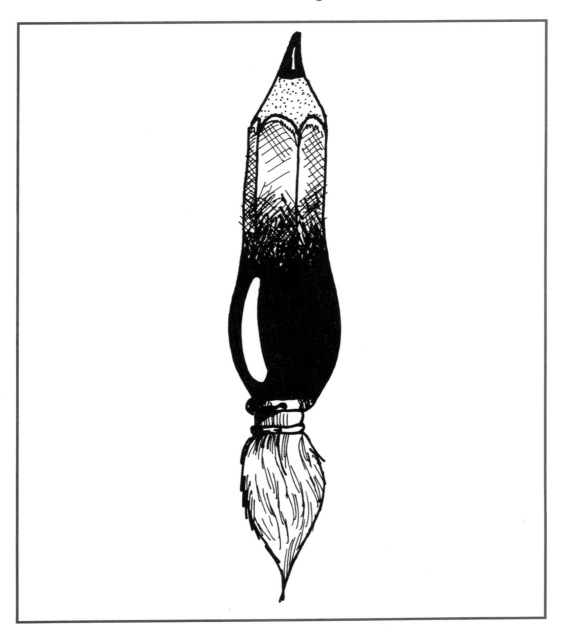

Drawing in various media

Most of the drawings you will have done so far will have been in pencil and pen. You might have tried a brush or two also. You can, of course, draw with just about anything that will make a mark on the paper surface. Try, for example, a home-made quill pen – a sharpened feather, your fingers, cocktail sticks and matchsticks, nibs cut from cardboard, bits of wire dipped in ink or bits of sponge.

Feel free to experiment: you might even discover a technique that sets your work apart from everyone else's.

Adding texture and shading

Adding texture and shading to your cartoons will give them more solidity. At the moment we are drawing 'open wire' figures. With shading these will become really three-dimensional.

In the example below I have shown objects without any shading, and then with shading to give them form.

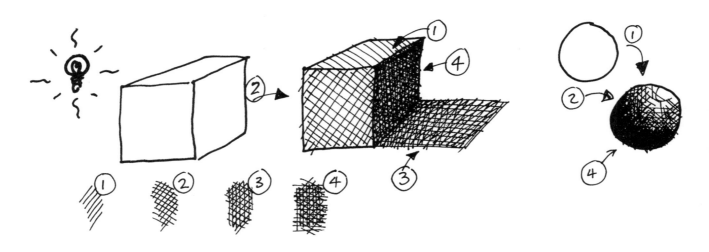

I draw a little light bulb to show where I have imagined the light is coming from. Place your shading in the area that will be in shadow and leave the illuminated area white. A curved surface is shaded so that the shading gradually gets lighter or darker as it comes into or out of the light.

Adding texture to your cartoons shows what the various things in it are made of. In these examples I have drawn a variety of surfaces. Try these for yourself, and maybe add a few of your own.

You don't need to fill your cartoon with shading or texture, or indeed to use any at all if you don't want to; but it is worth knowing how to do it all the same.

Lettering

Where a cartoon contains words, try to ensure that the words are clear and easy to read. It is also a good idea to check any spellings that you are uncertain of. Signs or instructions should be written in clear block capitals, as should any important parts of speech.

THESE WORDS ARE CLEAR...
these aren't so easy...
USE ALL CAPITALS, OR...
A Mixture Of Capitals
And Lower Case!

Normal speech should be written in clear 'normal' handwriting. 'Joined up' writing is not so easy to read, and so should be avoided unless it is very important to you that you have text set like that in your particular cartoon.

Make sure you plan and leave enough space for the words to fit into.

The examples below show hand lettered, computer printed and typewritten text.

When you are lettering by hand use pencil guide lines to help get the text in the right place before committing your deathless prose to ink. Don't be afraid to experiment with your lettering – but make sure that what you produce remains easy to read.

HAND DRAWN. HAND LETTERING CAN BE FANCY OR PLAIN....

TYPEWRITTEN TEXT CAN LOOK A BIT OLD FASHIONED THESE DAYS, BUT IS A CHEAP WAY OF DOING THE JOB!

Computers *can* produce a **wide range** of text styles and *sizes* and all YOU have to do is **glue** the _**printed**_ text onto your _**cartoon!**_

Remember that people generally read from left to right and from top to bottom, so make sure that your speeches follow each other logically. In the example below I have deliberately set the speech incorrectly – see how much more time it takes to work out what is happening.

Try to edit the words in your cartoons as much as possible. Keep sentences short, and never use a long word when a short one will do the job.

People spend very little time looking at cartoons – they are rarely studied in great detail – so to maintain attention you need to have a sharp drawing, focussed on the action, and snappy text.

ASSIGNMENT

Draw the same person, object and background in at least four different media. Add a variety of textures and tones to some of these drawings. Add some shading to make the things in your drawings look three-dimensional.

Now draw a cartoon using three different media in the one drawing. Photocopy this and add a variety of shading to each copy, you will soon learn what you enjoy doing and what comes most naturally to you.
Try out the methods of adding words described on page 50.

Now try this workout...

On a piece of paper draw a pen or pencil as realistically as possible, even adding a slight shadow to one side. Leave the sheet around somewhere and see if anyone is actually fooled into trying to pick it up and use it. If you take your time over the drawing I think you will be surprised at just how many people are fooled by it.

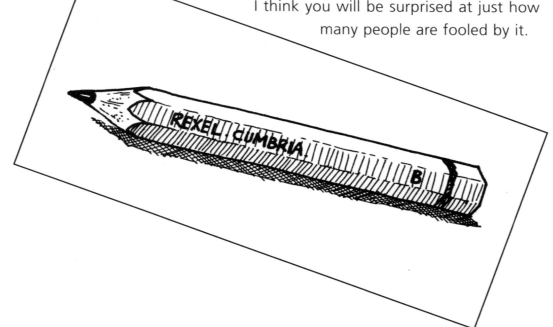

Caricature

Draw caricatures of yourself, friends and family.
Drawing from photographs, newspapers and TV.
Tips to make caricatures come to life.

Draw caricatures of yourself, friends and family

It is a good idea to start caricature with drawings of yourself. Having distorted your own features, and knowing how you feel about what you end up with, will help you to tackle other people.

Also, you can draw yourself from life (with a mirror) and from photographs, so you will be getting practice in drawing from the most often used sources.

A caricature is, to put it simply, a drawing of someone in which certain features or characteristics are exaggerated in order to make a humorous rather than lifelike image.

This does not mean that a rotten drawing with a big nose stuck on it will be a good caricature!

Some people find it easier to consider people as a collection of parts to begin with. Look at the shape of the head. Everyone is unique, of course, but there are very general shapes that you can use as a starting point. The same goes for noses, eyes and ears. All different, but certainly in groups.

I usually start a caricature with the eyes because I feel that the eyes have to look back at me when I am drawing. Then I work down the face via the nose and mouth, finally adding other details like hair, ears, accessories and dress.

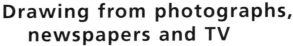

Little extras can make all the difference – hairstyles, mode of dress, facial hair, handbags, sunglasses and cigarettes can make a face that little bit more identifiable, which will certainly help with a 'slightly-less-than-perfect' likeness.

Don't be afraid to play Doctor Frankenstein and make your face up from successful bit and pieces – we all do it!

It sometimes helps to actually list (in words) the characteristics that make up a particular face. It is also useful to note that some caricatures work best from one angle or side.

Draw family and friends with care. Too much exaggeration can upset people and cause the wrong reaction to the rest of your cartooning endeavours!

Drawing from photographs, newspapers and TV

The chances of actually bumping into Cliff Richard and getting him to sit for a caricature are pretty remote, so you will often find yourself working from magazines or newspapers and TV when drawing the rich and famous.

Try to get a collection of pictures, rather than just one, so that you get a more balanced view of the 'victim', and are less likely to give them a double chin, when it was in reality just a shadow on one particular photograph. It has happened, believe me!

I routinely videotape political conventions and then make great use of the 'pause' button on the VCR to make sketches.

The personality-based magazines are good for collecting celebrity pictures, and they usually carry quite a few pictures of each person on a page, which is useful.

Tips to make caricatures come to life

If you get a good likeness and have added all the right accessories, you are well on your way to producing a really good caricature. What you need to remember, though, is that a caricature is like any other cartoon in one important respect – it has to have some action in there somewhere!

So don't just draw your caricatures standing there, looking out at you looking in at them. Give them something to do: put them in impossible situations, turn them into Martians, teapots, politicians or talking grandfather clocks, but get them at it!

Look at what other caricaturists are doing and adapt their ideas to begin with. You will have your own ideas eventually, but use theirs to get you started.

As long as you don't try to sell other people's ideas or otherwise pass them off as your own you will be on the right side of the copyright laws.

So stop worrying and start drawing.

Another good way to grab interest is to have your caricatures doing something they shouldn't be doing, or something that you might normally consider them never doing.

A caricature of someone famous washing up or scrubbing the floor is instantly more interesting than someone famous just sitting around being famous, because we want to know why this unusual thing is happening. Human curiosity is a wonderful thing, so put it to good use.

HE DIED FROM A SUDDEN ATTACK OF CURIOSITY!

ASSIGNMENT

Draw a caricature of yourself from the front and then from the side. Set up two mirrors to give you a reflection of the side of your face.

Draw caricatures of family and friends, using photographs to begin with and from life if people are happy to sit for you.

If people like their caricatures put them into a frame, sign them and give them away. Who knows, it might be the start of a whole new leisure pursuit or even part-time work for you!

Now try this workout...

Photocopy some newspaper photographs and paste your caricatures of the subjects over the heads in the photocopies. Ask the print shop to enlarge the copies to fill an A4 sheet to give you plenty of room to draw. Alternatively, have your caricatures reduced on a photocopier and add these to the newspaper pictures.

Strip cartoons
and Comics

How strip jokes work.
Introducing regular characters.
Different types of strip.
Writing strip scripts.

How strip jokes work

If you had to pick one phrase to describe the operation of a strip cartoon joke it would probably be 'delayed action.' The simplest format of a strip cartoon (and there are plenty of variations) consists of a joke introduced in box 1, the joke delayed or confused in some way in box 2, and a conclusion or punch line in box 3.

So, looking at the strip above we see the concept (which is a posh word for idea), the dog with no nose, introduced in the first box. In box 2 the idea is confused – (the ability of the dog to smell confused with his actual aroma – phew!). In box 3 the conclusion is reached...

This is a very simple example, but it forms the basis of many hundreds of published strip cartoons each and every year – look at a few and you will soon see the pattern developing.

Have a go for yourself. The ideas don't have to be terribly exciting and original at this stage, but just try a few out and see how it feels. Just remember, the formula is: CONCEPT – CONFUSION – CONCLUSION.

Sometimes there will be a part or parts of what is happening in the strip hidden from one or more of the characters; this often leads to misunderstanding, which can then be resolved in the final box. Do remember to keep back the punchline until the last possible moment – put it in the last words wherever you can, otherwise you end up with an "...Er..." at the end of the strip.

The exception to this 'rule' is a strip that you intend to draw on a regular basis, and here you can leave some questions unanswered and problems unresolved for the next strip. You should, however, deal with any unsolved items from the previous strip in this one, otherwise it will just become an unending series of unanswered questions!

Introducing regular characters

If you intend to introduce regular characters into your strip cartoons it is important that you spend time making them consistent. If the shape of the nose changes, or if they appear in different clothes for no apparent reason (and without warning by you) people will lose the essential 'belief' that makes the strip work.

Look at any successful long-running cartoon strip and take note of how the characters dress and how they look. Often they look the same now as they did 10, 20 or even 40 years ago.

For this reason I would advise anyone starting what they hope will be a long-running strip to produce character sheets for all the people (and things) that will appear in the strip. I would also recommend that you keep very fashionable people out of any strip that you want to produce for more than 6 months!

A character sheet should include front, back and side views of the characters, clothing details and information on backgrounds used in the cartoon. This can then be used as a reference source to ensure consistency.

There will be changes, naturally, as your own style changes and develops, but this will tend to take place over a number of months or years rather than between box 1 and box 2!

Different types of strip

Not all cartoon strips need to have the same characters. You can use a theme as the consistent factor and introduce whatever characters you need each time you draw the strip.

This is how most of my strips tend to work.

In the strip above I use the title bar to give a regular image to the strip, but I draw an entirely different 'cast' of people each month. You should try out both types of strip to begin with. You will soon get a feeling for what suits you best.

Writing strip scripts

If you asked 20 cartoonists how they write cartoon strips, you would get at least 21 different answers. Everyone works in a different way, but there are some general 'hints and tips' that might be of some use.

First, decide whether you think in pictures or in words. Most people have a preference for one or the other. Second, try to have some paper in front of you when you are having an idea-generating session. I know it sound obvious, but some people sit for hours 'trying to think up a joke idea' with nothing in front of them to write it down on when (or if) it ever finally appears.

The presence of paper will act as a prompt to your subconscious mind, setting it in action to produce something to actually go onto the paper!

If you have nothing in front of you your mind will simply assume that you aren't really serious, and so deliver little or nothing.

Try it: it really works!

I usually start with the words and write them into boxes right at the start. Then I add the rough layout. If I am happy that the idea will work I produce a quick pencil rough – to work out the placement of the figures, box sizes, etc. Then, when I have hopefully produced a dozen or so ideas, I put them away for a day or so and come back to them with fresh eyes.

If they are still reasonably funny (and it's amazing how unfunny a cartoon can get when you've gone through it 6 or 7 times!) I produce the final artwork.

Sometimes, even at this late stage, a modification or different approach will suggest itself, and my usual approach is to finish the drawing I have started and note down the other idea for later consideration.

ASSIGNMENT

Decide on a strip cartoon character and produce a character sheet for him or her or it! Then produce a couple of other characters to appear in the strip with them; they could be people, of course, or maybe a pet or a talking camera/TV/computer or something similar.

Draw up character sheets for these as well.

Think up a dozen strip cartoon scripts for these characters and then select two or three to draw up to a 'finished' standard.

Think up a theme for a cartoon strip using a variety of characters and produce scripts and finished drawings as above.

Now try this workout...

Take one of the finished strips from above and draw it with your other hand. If you are right-handed draw with your left, and vice versa.
No tracing is allowed!

Visual Cartoons

How to get a laugh without words.
Using signs and symbols.

How to get a laugh without words

A cartoon doesn't actually have to have any words in it to be funny. A well-drawn visual cartoon is like a mime act: the message is put across in visual signs and symbols.

We can, of course, cheat a bit and use actual signs and symbols until we get the hang of it, but the ultimate aim is to produce cartoons that are simply drawings and nothing else.

The easiest visual cartoons to draw are those which illustrate some point or other – in a slightly weird, wacky or strange way. So, for example, the door to a slimming club will, of course, be smaller where people come out than where they go in.

It will be perfectly natural for one house to display a sign saying 'drum kit for sale' and the house next door to be displaying a sign saying 'AT LAST'.

It is worth reminding yourself at this point that visual cartoons are not simply ordinary cartoons with the words rubbed out, although you can sometimes – by altering the drawing a little – convert an ordinary captioned cartoon to a visual cartoon.

You might even say that visual cartoons are a different kettle of fish!

Begin with signs – the 'Keep Off The Grass' cartoon has been popular with cartoonists for a good long time. Then there are the 'Silence', 'Bumps Ahead', 'Queue Here' and '5 items or less' signs that litter our streets and shops these days. Ask yourself questions about these signs.

How many ways are there to 'Keep Off The Grass'?

What method could you use to get around a 'No Parking' restriction?

Exactly what sort of bumps are there ahead?

When would it be appropriate not to keep silent in a library?

How would you get more than 7 items through a supermarket checkout?

This is a good opportunity to use the expressions and emotions in your cartoon people. If you can't use words to get your message across then use the acting ability of your characters – that's what you invented them for, after all!

Try some technical words from your hobby or employment to get the ball rolling. Put everyday objects into strange or inappropriate situations, or breathe life into otherwise inanimate objects, animals, even snails!

ASSIGNMENT

Pick half a dozen words or items connected with your work or hobbies, and draw them in such a way that they are being used for entirely the wrong purpose, or by the wrong people, or have been misinterpreted in some way. Remember that visual cartoons can be surrealistic and 'weird'.

A goldfish bowl might be worn by a deep sea diver, to keep water out instead of in. How about a railway carriage with guide dogs in it reading newspapers instead of their commuter owners? What sort of person would put their windscreen wipers on the inside windows of their car, and would it be sensible to sell central heating to people who live in Igloos?

Now try this workout...

Draw a cartoon using entirely straight lines – no curves of any kind allowed. Now draw with curves only – no straight lines this time.

Thinking up ideas

The four basic jokes.
Contrasts and misleading information.
Prop and jargon jokes.
The hidden element.
The cliche.
Collecting jokes.

The four basic jokes...

There are any number of jokes out there in the World, but as far as any comedian, cartoonist or humorist is concerned they can all be 'boiled down' to a given number of basic jokes; only the actual number will vary from individual to individual.

My own view is that there are four basic joke ideas, and these can be modified, mixed and mutilated sufficiently to produce an apparently endless supply of jokes for the cartoonist to use in an average lifetime.

Î will describe each idea in turn and give examples of how you might try approaching each with a view to producing jokes of your own.

Don't despair if you find this part of the cartooning business very hard – many other cartoonists do. Some cartoonists even give in and use specialist joke writers to produce the ideas, and they then simply (?) draw them.

It may well be that you could consider such a collaboration yourself. If you have a friend who is good at thinking up jokes, but not so good at drawing them, perhaps you could suggest working together.

Contrasts and misleading information

Think of all the things in the World that you can contrast with something else. Hot and cold, fast and slow, tall and short, clean and dirty, honest and corrupt, hard and soft, to name but a (very) few.

The contrast joke highlights these differences to make the humour.

Someone burgling an antique shop might well make their getaway in a horse-drawn carriage rather than a modern motor car. A contrast of old and new.

A lot of TV comedy sketches rely on this sort of contrast humour. I wrote a sketch myself which featured a group of cavemen struggling to make a wheel from a square lump of rock. Having failed completely to get anywhere, they all retired inside and helped themselves to a can of beer from a stone fridge and settled down to watch a stone TV set.

The contrast here was the inability of the cavemen to construct the wheel, set against the technologically advanced interior of the cave.

Misleading information is a similar notion, in that it relies on the contrast between what you thought was going to follow, and what actually did follow.

"I think love is the most important thing in a relationship, and I'm going to fall in love with the first millionaire I meet," is a cartoon caption using misleading information which suddenly changes direction half way through.

Or how about – "Of course there was a vacuum in my life when my wife left me, but she took that along with the video and dishwasher a week later."

Start with some simple phrases like "I love you terribly, Carol..." or "I like to help with the housework..." or "I never drink and drive..." and see what you can tack onto the end of it to mislead or act as a contrast.

It's a visual form of the 'Knock, Knock' joke, where you are given a word which then becomes someone's name in some odd way. You mislead with the first part of the joke...

...'Knock Knock'.....'Who's there?'..... 'Jim'.....'Jim who?'.....'Jim mind if I come in?'

This is a useful form of cartoon joke to use in a strip cartoon, where you have plenty of time to develop the joke idea, and introduce a delay. You can see the simple 'Knock, knock' joke as a cartoon strip without too much trouble.

Prop and jargon jokes

Imagine a magician sitting down to breakfast. He puts his top hat on the table and pours a bowl of cereal. When he has finished his cereal he snaps his fingers and his toast pops out of the top hat.

This is a prop joke. It uses a magician's prop (top hat) and changes its use so that we get toast instead of a rabbit. In the same way a tired brain surgeon might put his coat on back to front when he leaves to go home.

In this category we can use visual material a lot more. Someone spinning rapidly round and round could simply have got his battery-powered screwdriver stuck in a tight screw, for example. We have to accept, of course, that it is physically impossible to achieve, but

that is what being a cartoonist is all about!

Think of all the props that you use in your everyday life, and think up some crazy combinations or bogus new uses for them. Compare the real use to the made-up use you've just thought of – maybe there is another cartoon idea in there, too?

Now consider jargon – technical words that mean something sensible to regular users; but that doesn't mean we have to take them seriously.

Do photographers really test fisheye lenses by dropping them into a tank of water?

Is hard water a window cleaner's dropped bucket landing on someone's head?

In archery they use a quiver; some photographers use zoom lenses suggesting, of course, the noise they make when you drop them from the top of a tall building; a laptop that's a bit too user friendly might be a problem if you're wearing a short skirt; a topless bar might be where bald men go!

When you start to think about the possibilities for prop and jargon jokes you will soon find ideas coming thick and fast – or is that just a stupid racing driver?

The hidden element

In a joke like this there is something that can either be seen only by you or is hidden from one or more of the cartoon characters. For example, we might have a drawing of a man dragging himself onto a desert island, but not being able to see the sign saying 'Quicksand' that we can see on the other side of the island.

Imagine two people in a room talking about a third person who is out of sight in another room.

One says to the other, "He watches neighbours every night." In the other room, that only we can see, is a very shifty-looking individual peering through a telescope.

An astronaut picking a small flower on the surface of another planet will be unaware of the giant version of the same plant standing behind him brandishing a large club; possibly the club will be shaped like another astronaut?

The cliché

When all else fails it's time to head back to known, tried and tested ground; the cliché. Take a desert island, a doctor's waiting room, a courtroom, a king's jester in cap and bells, a baby in a pram or buggy, or a psychiatrist's couch.

You can start by making a sketch of the situation just to see if anything flashes into your mind, or maybe break it up into components and fiddle around with them individually.

A man could have a huge desert island style palm tree, carved into the shape of a young woman, crammed into his suburban bedroom; his wife insists "Something happened to you on that island, didn't it, Geoff?" Or maybe a desert island covered in bottles (all filled with messages) and a sign saying 'BOTTLE BANK'. Or just a man, clearly alone, on a desert island, saying 'I'm worried about Frank, he's started talking to himself'.

Even if nothing comes to mind, you will still be getting some valuable drawing practice!

Try also clichéd phrases like 'Take us to your leader,' or 'It's just a phase he's going through,' or 'You and whose army?'. Try to imagine who is saying them, to whom and why and see what you can come up with.

Try the litter method. Write names, places, things, punchlines, or anything else you fancy onto slips of paper. Throw them in a heap on the desk or floor and pick up a few at random and see what you can do with the resulting set of words.

Collecting jokes

It is a good idea to collect jokes and cartoons, either as words in a notebook or as tear-outs from newspapers and magazines, or both.

You will soon start to see how certain jokes are put together, or at least what type of joke idea they spring from.

You will have a favourite kind of joke, even a favourite cartoonist, and if you study their cartoons you should see what kind of jokes they prefer to draw.

Allow – never force – your own peculiar sense of humour and drawing style to develop, and never try to draw cartoons 'like' someone else.

It is fairly easy to copy someone else's drawing style, but there is absolutely no reason to do it. Your cartoons are unique, just as you are, and you should be proud of what you produce.

ASSIGNMENT

Think up two jokes for each of the categories described in the last chapter, and then draw them. Decide which is your favourite type of joke, and try to think up twenty jokes for this category. Draw up half a dozen of these ideas.

Try and think up a new cliche joke every day, as well as at least half a dozen general joke ideas.

Now try this workout...

Collect 50 cartoons from newspapers. Remove the captions and paste them into a notebook. Paste the drawings into a scrapbook. Go through both books at regular intervals and think up new captions for each cartoon, and new drawings for each caption.

Glossary of cartooning terms and technical information

Everything you need to know about
cartooning, and some other stuff that
I wanted to get off my desk as well.

Artwork The finished drawing. This is what it's all about!

Animation Moving cartoons, achieved by showing a number of still pictures (called frames) very quickly, so that the brain doesn't register each frame individually, but sees them as moving.

A4 Paper is measured in European A sizes. A4 is twice the size of A5. A3 is twice the size of A4.

Caricature A portrait drawing which is deliberately exaggerated for humorous effect. Often used in topical and political cartooning.

Cartoon Originally the term meant 'a preliminary sketch for a painting' but now it embraces almost any drawing that doesn't fit neatly into a traditional category.

Character sheet A sheet of drawings showing the characters regularly appearing in comics and strip cartoons, so that a consistent likeness can be achieved. Especially useful where a strip will have several different artists over its lifetime, as is the case with long-running comics. Sometimes called a 'dope sheet'.

Cliché A cartoon situation that has been used many times by a number of different artists. The shipwrecked person on a desert island is probably the most well-known example.

Comic A cartoon book in the form of a newspaper. Usually thought to be for children only, but many comics are read by people of all ages.

Fee The agreed amount that will be paid for a cartoon when drawn for publication or for a client. This is usually agreed in advance, sometimes after a sketch has been submitted.

Fugitive The word used to describe inks or paints that fade over a period of time. Some companies use permanence ratings to give an idea of the likely life of their products.

gsm The weight of paper. The amount of pulp in grams required to make up one square metre of paper. Typing and photocopying paper is usually 80 gsm; watercolour paper can be 300 gsm or even more.

India ink A waterproof drawing ink. It contains shellac and should not be used in fountain pens, as the ink will dry out and completely block the pen. A version of India ink for fountain pens is available.

Media The general term for drawing and painting materials.

Props Things that are added to a cartoon to give the characters something to do or to introduce a joke idea or to show what is happening.

Rough or visual a quick drawing done to show how things will be arranged in a final cartoon; a sketch.

Sable An expensive material used in high quality brush making. Sable brushes hold more liquid than nylon equivalents, and usually last longer.

Stereotypes Images of groups or types of people. A burglar in a striped jersey is a stereotype, as such a person doesn't really exist. Good cartoonists never need to use sexist, racist or other forms of hurtful stereotypes.

Technical pen A pen which has a fine metal tube for a nib, and produces a consistent and even line for drawing. Technical pens can be expensive, but with care should last many years.

Visual See Rough above.

You The most important person in the whole cartooning process, without whom none of what is about to happen could happen. Good Luck!

Sadly, that brings us to the end of *'How To Draw Cartoons'.*

I hope that you have enjoyed working through this book as much as I have enjoyed writing and illustrating it, and I also hope that some of what you have read has inspired you to grab a pencil and have a try at cartooning for yourself.

You don't need any special materials, equipment, qualifications or experience to draw cartoons; anyone can do it.

You are never too young or too old to draw cartoons, and it doesn't matter what sex, height, race, religion, creed or colour you are: everyone can learn 'How To Draw Cartoons'.